Every Broken Little Thing

Poems by Adrian Lime

Luchador Press
Big Tuna, TX

Copyright © Adrian Lime, 2021
First Edition: 1 3 5 7 9 10 8 6 4 2
ISBN: 978-1-952411-88-5
LCCN: 2021950620

Cover art: Rob W. Jones
Author photo: Jonie McIntire
All rights reserved. No part of this publication may be reproduced or transmitted in any form or by any means, electronic or mechanical, including photocopying, recording or by info retrieval system, without prior written permission from the author.

Acknowledgments:

The author would like to thank the editors of these publications where some of these poems were previously published:

Bards Again 2016 (The Poetry Barn): "A Trip to the Zoo," "Background Files," "Force of Habit,"

Feeding the Monster (EMP Books): "Adjustments," "Gap in the Line!"

Glass Streets: a poetry anthology from Toledo Streets Newspaper: "Times to Remember,"

Red Fez, online literary journal: "Athanor," "Breakthrough,"

Remembrance Anthology — Worcestershire Poet Laureate Nina Lewis: "I Remember"

*Tuesday Night at Sam and Andy's Uptown Café (*Westron Press): "What We Will Do," "Beat Dog Poetry"

TABLE OF CONTENTS

The House of Poetry / 1

Buzzards / 2

I Am Teaching My Son How to Make Fire / 3

Sometimes the Poem / 5

Times to Remember / 6

A Wolf in My Stomach / 9

Winter in Havana / 10

Xanadu's Now, Man! / 12

Beat Dog Poetry / 13

from Walking in Toledo (1995-1996) / 15

What We Will Do / 22

One Lucky Bastard / 24

Boy Games / 26

Prayers for Timmie / 29

Poetry Submission / 31

The Big Reveal / 32

Autumn Sounds / 34

On Allen Ginsberg's Death / 37

Tiny Dirges / 38

Matin for My Wife / 42

Even When You've Hidden / 43

The Mathematics of Talking about Love / 44

Don't Fear the Easy Path / 45

Every Broken Little Thing / 46

Breakthrough / 49

Adjustments / 51

Gap in the Line! / 52

Fugue / 54

Background Files / 57

In Fire Times / 59

Lori Listening to Sarah Vaughan / 61

Soirée / 62

While Leaves Fall in Autumn / 63

Love Poems / 64

Ode to Our Blue Curtain / 65

The Best Poets I Know Are Workers / 67

The Bumblebee and the Falcon / 69

Force of Habit / 70

The Barcode on Your Head / 71

Two Birds / 73

Keeper of the Loaves / 78

Horses and Art in the Age of COVID-19 / 79

To Rhyme a Poem / 81

Two Drunken Poems Composed by a Tree / 82

This Is not a Pipe / 83

Dr. Don Bop / 85

Why I Write Poetry / 87

Athanor / 91

I Remember / 93

A Trip to the Zoo / 95

Love Is Something Like Hot Sauce / 97

Myole Corona / 99

The Bird Shit Cleaners / 100

Family Secrets / 102

After Reading Ted Kooser All Night at Work / 103

Lady on the Condom Machine / 104

Perfection / 107

I Can Feel It / 109

Unsolicited Advice for Insecure People / 113

To Jonie, Kerry, and Michael

Every Broken Little Thing

The House of Poetry

Don't wipe your hands on a rag
before taking up your pen.
Don't brush off your boots
before entering the house of poetry.

The grease from the factory,
the soil from the field—
they are part of the poem.

Buzzards

Summer days when I woke up to heat
and scent of manure, clouds so thin
they weren't clouds, just helpless
attempts to block the sun, I saw

eagles playing the air like music
so high above the fields. And standing
as I watched them soar, the farmer, who I helped
hay the cattle, simply said *buzzards*.

It didn't matter. I was eight, and they
were huge and lovely and smooth in the sky. And I
thought of being up there with them as each
bale tumbled from the back of the hay

wagon. Until we came upon the lamb
that had fallen into a drainage gulley
some days before, surrounded by cloaked
figures of death fighting for pieces,

only frightened off for a moment when
the farmer shouted *hyahh git!* to see
if it was a calf. Then they bounded
back with ragged wings spread

and suddenly I felt
the heat all around me
and stopped looking up.

I Am Teaching My Son How to Make Fire

It begins with a piece of charred cotton,
a small nest of dry grass,
and a spark.

I tell him, you don't make fire—
you give it a spark, and you feed it.
You feed it the air
and it makes its own fire.
You don't blow too hard
or you could blow it out.

Our faces pitch down near
the small nest in my cupped hands,
I blow lightly, coaxing the spark to spread
and it spreads, orange glow stretching
across black cotton, then
a tiny spindle of smoke—

Watch, I say.
And the spark turns
into a tiny ball of flame.

I drop this new fire into
a pile of twigs we had prepared,
and I tell him,
*Now you must grunt and say,
'Ugg... Men make fire!'*

I see my wife and daughter
walking with fishing poles to the pond—
so I say to him
And women make men...
so who really makes fire?

My son says,
We make fire.

Sometimes the Poem

Sometimes the poem is your older brother,
an exasperating love you can't imagine losing.
Sometimes the poem is your older brother— always there
for you when you need him most, but then
he beats your ass for no good reason.

Sometimes the poem is your lover
you've waited a seeming lifetime to hold
and now that she's here you can't get enough.
Sometimes the poem is your lover and nothing else
in the world exists at that very moment.

Sometimes the poem is your dog, impatiently
waiting for you to just throw the stick already.
Sometimes the poem is your old drinkin' buddy.
Maybe too often the poem is your old drinkin' buddy.
Both have seen you at your worst and still hang around.

And sometimes the poem is a swallowed fish hook—
a silver treble, triple-barbed to stay put, to sink in deep,
to hold tight no matter how hard you fight at that line—
and all you're left to ask yourself just then is
what are you willing to go through to get it out?

Times to Remember

My sister sent me a notebook,
200 pages bound in marbled leather
top edge gilt, inscribed with
a Navajo proverb. Beautiful.
She wrote a message to me on the inside cover
telling me that she loves me
that she hopes I fill it with poems—
a Christmas gift 1992.

I haven't written in it yet because
I haven't yet filled my other notebooks—
those, too, given to me
by others who love me,
or those notebooks I've found, cheap
with curling pages, glue and plastic.

And there are those times
when I'm prime for this world,
when music brings out words in my head,
times when my car is enough
to bring out the words,
or the moon is enough,
or the babbling stink
of the Maumee river
or the happy song
of the purple lady on Cherry Street
are enough to bring out words.

There are times when it's easy
and I open up and flow—
times when I can recall things in safety,
let them just spill out of me
onto paper.

But then there are those times
when the ink that runs
could as easily be blood,
when I gravely clutch at my pen
like holding a nail,
times when the only people I see
plod through nighttime streets
like dirty diesel machines.
Times the night is darker,
the days are darker,
times when the ink is blood and is wine,
when the pen is the nail
and I have to scratch it hard onto paper
or just run away because I'm no Jesus.

There are times when ink pens are luxuries—
let us not forget these times either—
times when death grabbed our friends
with intimate words and they leapt for safety
into some nightmare anonymous—
there are those times to find yourself
under bridges where desperate people go
to do desperate things.

These are the times to start new notebooks.
These are the times to remember, because
not everyone makes it back—
not everyone finds himself
eventually back to safety
where family is free
to send gifts and blessings.
These are the times
when a hot cup of coffee
didn't just save your ass
from freezing on the pavement.

A Wolf in My Stomach

Another day gone by
        counting change
without a bite to eat.
One of these days I'm going to
learn how to take care of myself.
For now, at least, I go hungry.

It makes me sick watching people eat,
nibbling french fries at every meal
        (in fast food joints, on street corners).
My stomach turns, uneasy. I
yawn, leave the restaurant empty.

Some day I know I'll learn
to just drop my head and eat like an
old horse at a trough. I will
munch my fries like everyone else,
and probably learn to like it. But today I'll
count my change and watch all the others,
hungry as hell, but too sick to care.

Winter in Havana

for Carlos Guietti

I took a taxi from the hospital in Havana—
I'd been a stranger too long,
so I ran crazed through a street fair
cackling like a mynah bird
>and then fell to my knees
silent as a tractor with no spark plug.
They put me in an asylum for two days.
I told them *I'm American*
>they threatened never to let me out.

I crept back to the room
I rented from Mrs. Guietti.
>The money in my jeans was taken,
so I ran some down to the taxi driver
who seemed happy to wait—
he was happy to be paid—
>Mrs. Guietti was happy I was back.

It's December and the kitchen
smells like cinnamon.
I want to eat a tomato and a nectarine
>I settle for a cup of chili beans
a piece of dry flat bread
a glass of beer.
>I yawn, and my eye catches sight
of the Mother Mary, a copper statuette

          even cast of metal her face is soft.
I would like a handful of raisins
but we have no raisins.

I walk into the street,
December is the best time of year
no rain and not too hot.
A breeze pulls sweat across my face
          the scent of a dead cat somewhere.
When I close my eyes
I could be in New York City—
I could be in any big city—
the whir and mumble of people,
the whir and crash of the city—

In the day, I can close my eyes
but at night, the night changes everything—
there's music and alcohol and
Carlos and I wind through the streets
throwing stones at stray cats
and more stray cats,
and Mrs. Guietti worries
          about the police.
There's always the fear of the police.

Xanadu's *Now*, Man!

for Nick Muska
a translitic from a Vietnamese poem, by Sa Nho

Xanadu, man. *Xanadu!* Think about this
behind your tryingly grey eyes. Xanadu, man— it
may be trying to quietly call us all home there.
Trying, eh?! Sacks hang in shrubs there,
full of fruit for the mouth!

You bet I'm gonna die trying to go.
Listen, man, Timbo can laugh all he wants
that mindless boob—
Man, Xanadu is *now!* Can dig? *Now!*
Don't just think I'm tokin' my bong.

Look, look, I'm trying to draw a triangle,
a triangle drawn in the gaps,
a triangle in the maps to get us there,
Trying, eh?!
We gonna go. We gonna go.
I'm trying to draw it in,
are you trying too?

Beat Dog Poetry

for the Almeda Street Poets

We're beat dogs.
Beat into the ground
beat with leash and collar
beat from work fatigue,
beat from bad wine and
good coffee rot gut.
We're called Ginsbergian posers
by some who were beat themselves once
and envy the new shit-on fresh beat.
We're bushed-beat,
we're bramble-beat,
we're beat-beatific-beautiful.
We may listen to Marley,
we may listen to Nat King Cole,
we may listen to Gershwin and Rachmaninov,
we may listen to Bach and Brahms and Beethoven,
Janis and Jefferson and Jimi,
but we always listen to each other.
When we're beat once,
we're beat again—
we beat each other,
we beat ourselves bloody.
We beat our poetry,
we beat our poems in coffee shops
on rooftops, street corners, county fairs
and elementary schools.

We're beat out of society
and beat right back in—
beat up, beat down, beat in, beat on, beat through,
beat all the other prepositions and then a few—
this new beat is nothing new.

Beat beat beat—
have we said it enough, beat beat?
We're saying we're beat—
hep cat, beat dog,
blueberry morning people of the sun,
and that motionless MacLeish moon—
our poems do not mean, but beat.
We're beat like all before
and all who'll follow,
we're beat now
and we're beat tomorrow,
but as long as we're beat together
we're still us, a weird generation,
we are a barking pack of beat dogs
and these poems,
these poems are our howls.

from Walking in Toledo (1995-1996)

One
With camera in hand
I walk down streets
in the night,
dim-lit white globes in mist
bending over street corner curbs
onto endless brick and steel
reflections on storefront windows
dusty as they are, but still
pulsing the nights' flashing lights

Another
Walking down Secor Road
under train track bridge
I kicked snow off of years ago
contemplating depression and hunger
quarter of four in the morning
headache and tired knees
I've got much further to go and
many fast cars are out

Another
Not much to do tonight
out of the coffee shop, closed
wandering around snapping photos
shots of shadows on roads' curves
rusted staples in porous telephone poles

all these power cables bending
and light glint reflections scooting down
in motion with the wind

Another
There's a certain walk
that goes with knowing where you are
and no one else can find you
late in dark parts
and it's too cold to cry
a sullen strut knowing
the frustrations of those
maybe looking for you
but you could be anywhere

Another
When you get a pebble in your boot
it's important to get it out
right away—
you could be contemplating murder
or suicide,
but god damn
if that pebble doesn't stay
at the front of your mind
everywhere you go till it's gone

Another
Listen to the crazies
at night
alone as you are

everywhere
they've got something to say
and few to hear them
and you've got few
to listen to

Another
I never noticed
the little woman
light brown skin white hair
at the bus stop bench
corner of Byrne and Dorr
but she's been there
the last five days morning night
every time I've passed
always singing something to herself

Another
After hours of walking
and fatigue-thinking
with sting of winter air, but
your breath warms your face
anyhow against breeze, these
leaves start to have voices
and walking on gravel—
there's a sweet sound to gravel
under foot when no one's around

Another
Lori's married in Chicago

having a child
Andrew's moving to Colorado
to find himself in a bong
Ann will be all over the country
always driving
and here I'll still be walking
always writing

Another
When smoke-air stings your eyes
and brings out slow tears
and smokestacks hide the moon
and salt-dusted cars squeal on pavement
when the Maumee River is ice-covered
but still stinking and sirens
are distant but everywhere
you've got to know that you're home

Another
Down past fenced lumberyard
with razored wires on top
and two black dogs barking
pawing the crooked fence toward me
I snapped a picture of them
four inches from wet mouths making them
bark even louder. They were angry
with bad breath, then I walked on
and they just sat there looking

Another
Walking past Central toward Sylvania Ave
to Betsy Ross' for some coffee
and stopped by Donald M at a BP
where he spat twice on a handkerchief
and polished a spot on his car
and told me how to get to
two more readings
in happenin' places I can't miss

Another
Past long grey white-corroded chainlink
U-Lock-It slumps a man
green combat jacket
hands pocketed
dark pits of eyes on dark skin
tired face and few teeth
blue knit toque pulled low to eyebrows
smiles at me, bright HELLO!
eyes still circling, searching

Another
Red old iron beams and chicken wire
three-beamed greenbrown wood
slant-cut triangular rough rails
fitted into fat posts in the ground
fences everywhere!
surrounding buildings houses pets
people rivers streets Keep Out!
blue security lights blink
but gaping gates at every factory

red lights spin— beware
driver cannot see you

Another
Down past wide-windowed hall where I once
stole half a cake from trash can
now bright with concert people schmoozing
early evening, early stars peeking
past street lights blinking awake
blue moon hangs by streetlamp
makes my face glow looking in
to their warmth and music, hungry
and a few wine-glassed eyes see anything
in the window but their own reflections

Another
Dark man in trench coat
at building corner of defunct mall
strumming unpowered electric guitar
eyes closed, tapping foot
throwing down his whole leg to it
fast-paced and crooked fingers
asks me for a cigarette
I sit a little happy
and smoke with him

Another
Yellow monkey fist of crane arm
swings impossibly long brown pole
over head of helmeted woman who

puts gloves up to guide it
spinning the whole thing gently around
like it was nothing. She has strong hands
pulls fatter end of huge pole
touching it to the ground presses it in place
shouts *Yep!*

What We Will Do

We will share coffee on cold mornings
and poke our fingers into the steam
We will drink
and say, *It tastes good*
We will enjoy ourselves
and one another

We will wear warm clothes and take walks
wool socks and long johns
We will pull red leaves from trees
and make piles of them, precariously high,
then we'll kick them over

We will have pets, and some pets will run away—
those that don't will die
at ripe old ages
with arthritic shoulders
that we will rub when they nuzzle us

We will barbecue in Autumn.

We will walk on cliffs' edges
and swim in oceans
We will remark how steep the cliffs are
how cold the water
We will feel things with our fingers

We will attend funerals
and we'll say, *God rest their souls*
We will pay our respects,
then we'll play

We will converse without speaking
touch each others' eyelids
We will lie down,
tangle our legs together
whisper with our fingers

We will eat peaches.

One Lucky Bastard

I've wound my way through endless halls
with wood-paneled walls,
so much frosted glass and brass trim.
I've been helped through security checkpoints
to floor sixteen where cards are swiped
and thick glass doors buzzed open—
I've traversed vast expanses of
fabric-covered fields of cubical—
a latticework of uniformity, like fractal corals
spread beneath perfect humming fluorescence.

I am lost and desperate in a foreign land,
my wife's office building.
I am just to drop off a letter, something important
she meant to bring with her.
Can you drop it off quick on your way to work?
Sure— I'll meet you up there.

My factory life makes sense to me, but
this sterile place is horrifying. It's too quiet,
everyone smiles pleading smiles, and all the air
smells like toner and carpet shampoo.

Just then, passing the far end
of the aisle I'm currently trapped in,
she crosses my line of sight. On some task, I'm sure, but
she doesn't know I'm there. She is in her element

and I'm doe-eyed, fumbling and hopeless.
She is the most beautiful person I've ever laid eyes on,
and I am one lucky bastard.

It reminds me of years back
when we were students together,
crossing paths in university halls,
hoping to match up our schedules,
keeping my eye out for her, wishing
to bump into her at unexpected moments,
making time to meet at coffee shops,
wholly unaware of what the future held for us.
I didn't have the eyes back then
to see the woman I see today.

I hear her voice rise from some submerged place
some workspace hidden in a matrix of sameness,
say, *He's here? Right now?* And her head pops up,
she is standing tippy-toe, a quick sweep and she finds me.
I hold up the envelope and wave— and she smiles—
she smiles at me like I'm some kind of hero.

Boy Games

My hand slips and I bust a knuckle
on an engine block.
I wave my hand like it's on fire
and laugh a little,
not because it doesn't hurt—
it does—
I laugh at the memory of my brother and I
punching our fists together as a game.
You hold yours still, and I get a hit.
I hold mine still, and you get a hit.
Each time it hurt us both like hell, but
we had to see who would quit first.
Knuckles bloodied and
waving the hand like it's on fire.

I always lost *bloody knuckles*. Never once won.
I wasn't very good at boy games.

When we were younger, a local farmer
used our back acres to grow feed corn.
And at end of summer, the corn harvested,
the back acres littered with errant ears of hard,
dry corncobs scattered over the vast field—
my brother and I played a game of throwing
these hard, dry corncobs at each other
just as fast as we could.

Now understand, this was a game
wherein the rules and ultimate goal
were simply to throw corncobs at each other
just as fast as we could.
That was the game, nothing else.

There were always bruises.
There was always blood.
Best hit wins. Honor system.
That was the rule.

And to this day, as a grown man
as a father of sons, I fear
the boy games my sons must get into,
but when my mind wanders back,
I remember my best day— the day I won.

The day my brother, after dodging a corncob
past his head at breakneck speed, pried up
a cornstalk root ball, heavy with hardened clay,
a monkey-fist of gnarled root and rock, and he heaved it
with all his might over his shoulder
like a shot put, sweat trailing through dust
on his child's face, and shouted *Grenade!*

And I proved my mettle by standing stock still—
hunker down and take the hit.
I didn't move an inch until the entire weight of it
whomped my back, echoed hollow through my lungs,
and I arched and screamed, swiping at my back

for the root ball that had already
toppled to the ground.

I hadn't moved. I won.
My brother running to me, yelling
Oh my God! I'm so sorry!
Why didn't you move?

There were always bruises.
There was always blood.
Best hit wins. Honor system.
That was the rule.

Prayers for Timmie

I played Star Wars in the climbing tree
outside our farmland ranch house.
The tree, a real place of refuge.
Three low branches converged in just such a way
as to become the cockpit of an X-Wing fighter.
And I shouted commands, barrel-rolled
through space, squeaking pew-pew-pew
with a voice not yet deepened with age.

That silver maple tree I climbed so many times
to escape punishment, to hide from my older brother,
to search for robins' nests,
to enter my imagined worlds—
and being adept at climbing that tree so fast,
to escape the jaws of the menacing
German shepherd who often broke his rope
and ran wild through his country block territory.

This German shepherd was a true terrorizer,
an irregular visitor but constant fear, most infamous
for chasing down Ricky Crites as our
backyard football game quickly broke up,
and biting him in the ass. We all scattered,
and Ricky ran like hell, fast for a ten-year-old—
but not fast enough. Mr. Crites
came out from his house with a rifle,
fired it into the air, and that beast of a dog
ran off, one bloody ass cheek in his wake.

The German shepherd's name,
as God is my witness,
was Timmie.
Timmie the ass-biting German shepherd.

I ran like lightning home, and
fearing for my own ass, flew up
that Star Wars tree like it was nothing.
I hugged tight to a limb half-way up, quivering
afraid of Timmie from the ground,
afraid that Mr. Crites's bullet would
drop back down from the sky
and hit me in the head.

But each night, at bedtime prayers,
I prayed that God would watch over Timmie,
keep him safe as he hunkered down all alone,
tied with a frayed rope to his shamble doghouse
all night in windy rain.

No one should live like that. Nor dog either.
Not even Timmie.
But also, as sweetly as I could, I prayed
that the Lord Above would please
convince Timmie not to bite our asses.

There was fun to be had, games to be played,
TIE-fighters to fight, footballs to be thrown,
but there was no place
no place for the biting of asses.

Poetry Submission

It's tough, you know
letting your little metaphor
wander off on his own
without so much as a note
safety-pinned to his lapel.

Like dropping him off
at the school bus stop
his first day of kindergarten,
        worrying,
what will the others think of him
how will he find his way?

The Big Reveal

for Skyler

I know that it's wrong to describe this news
as, let's say, a bedspread being suddenly pulled off
from atop my Jack Russell who was sweetly curled
like a cashew in that warm alcove behind my knees
in our morning bed. The medley of fatigue and surprise—
shock at the onrush of cold and light— the big reveal when
our bedspread draws back and we say *why now?* But
it's morning, and, really, we both know it is time to rise.

It isn't the pitiless, unending return of tsunami water that
follows after a beach is first drawn bare, the water pulled back
by the growing wave, receded more than a mile horizon-ward
as head-scratching onlookers begin walking out, much too far,
onto the slick decline that was, until so recently, seafloor.
It must be intriguing, yes, but some natural thing in them
must also suspect that the water would return— that
the void would again fill in, and swallow them with it.

It is self-deception even to hint at surprise— shock at the news
of your transfer today to hospice, to deny further treatment.
The big reveal on Christmas Eve day for Christ's sake—
the timing of this, if we're honest, is perfectly like you.
Only, I could've as easily flipped open a calendar, stabbed
my finger onto any square and hollered *why this day of all days!*

I know it's wrong, I know it's lazy, but it's all I have.
So the bedspread slides off,
all that tide-water returns,
a big red X on this calendar page
and here I still remain minus you.

Autumn Sounds

They were simple sounds
we heard from far away
the air cool,
and so tall the hills—
morning sun, our shadows
thrown long in the
low-light chirr of sun up.

We walked close, the
slaughterhouse standing deep grey
in the hung dust of morning fog—
we walked closer, the faint smells
now echoing down the hill
growing sharper
but up we went in our skin
in our full bodies grown large
in our world ripe and round—

Frost turned to dew beneath
autumn's morning moon
the shadow of the slaughterhouse
above us all as we reached it.
Those curious looks on the faces
of my children, shining
leaning against the wall
listening through the wall
to those autumn sounds.

The sounds had drawn us up the hill,
but the smell that morning
like wet steel and must—
the smell drew them to the door
to peek through, their shining faces
their child's eyes.

My loves,
        their faces now gone mute,
muffled breaths of white steam
quick through gaped mouths
as, inside, lines of lambs and pigs,
pigs they had ridden in summer
hung inverted in lines
efficiently straight
hooves strapped together
gutted, ribcages exposed
like bloody harps.
Mouths wide,
soundless.

It's been a good year.
I said.

My children stood weak-kneed
at the slaughterhouse door—
the autumn sun cresting the hills,
sweeping the fog back to the sky.
We returned to the house quietly
but for the rhythmic trudge

through knee-deep wet grass.
I watched their faces, and they
watched their feet.

Some thoughts have nowhere to go, but
you can hear them on autumn mornings.

Next summer, when my children
feed the pigs and clean their pens,
they will do so thoughtfully,
they will remember why our bodies
have grown larger, fuller
they will keep quiet count of time,
keep count of its worth.

On Allen Ginsberg's Death

The first shock of what a poem can do
is a precious gift, and no need to know
to whom you've given it.

I saw you read for an hour in Michigan
and you swore your only wish in your old age
is that your asshole holds out.

Your poems were soft and loud, sounded nothing
like slow swell of a siren on an East Village street
driving to collect your silent mouth, still body.

But if we would've been together that day
I would've offered to hold you, carry you
in my arms like a child.

And when the great dark figure walked with us
touching your heart, squeezing your breath,
you alone would've seen him there.

And when newspaper clippings wrapped their black
on you, telephones ringing all over the country
have you heard? and I staggered for a moment,

some part of you reached out from your books
from that sullen place, reached out to me,
offered to carry me in your arms like a child.

Tiny Dirges

Like a late frost lays
on a young bud
I do not fear death,
but I know better than
to cling to life.

I want to right the wrongs
I know are wrong right now
so I can recognize my final moment
when it comes.

This world has a way to push you
into exhausted silence
but silence is already a kind of death.

Every man in my family has died
relatively young, around age 60—
complications of the heart.
I accept this like a well-worn slipper.

Too poor to go to the ER for each chest pain,
so my death will be the indigestion
that wasn't indigestion.
To be fair, most of the time
it was indigestion.

I want to find those things
that I'll be ashamed of
when my final moment comes
and fix them now—
more than anything, I fear
my own shame.

My figure of death will be wearing
knee-socks with a hole in the toe.

I do not want my children
to have children so I can be a grandfather
to pass on my genes—
I want my children to have children
so they can fully understand love.

I have no interest
in passing a torch.

Every cemetery is a model—
The wealthy are on the hill
with monuments of marble.
The working class are numerous
with stones to commemorate
the moving of stones.
The poor lay low in fields,
sodden, when the rain comes.

There are thirteen people
I hope come to my funeral.

My figure of death
pulls his cloak tight
to hide his comb-over.

I feel like all of my friends
are dying of cancer,
but this is not true.
Most of my friends are alive and healthy.

I want my friends to stop
dying of cancer.

I want to finish writing one book
before I die.

I'd like to finish writing five books
before I die.

Really, it's a matter of
how many books I finish writing
before I die.

It took me twelve years
to forget the real sound
of my father's voice.

This contract of life is broadly written
and you were never consulted
when it was made,
but there's your name
on the bottom line.

It's too late for me
to die pretty,
so I hope I die
old.

Although I don't fear death today,
I'm sure that fear will find me
when my final moment comes, and

I only hope, above all else—
beyond all of my sins and mistakes,
beyond all my grievances and restitutions,
that when people think of me,
they will think of kindness.

Matin for My Wife

Let our eyes open each morning
    our first vision each other

Let our hands brush together
    beneath the kitchen table

Let me find the perfect color
    for your coffee

Let us remember the sun
Let us remember the rain

Let my hard hands never
    be too hard to hold

Let our arguments be for no good reason
    Let us kiss and make up

Let us be water and stone
    fire and earth

Let this day bring what it will
Let us see it through together

Even When You've Hidden

yourself from your friends
beneath the warped porch boards
because no one understands
what you mean,
no one understands
what you meant

something remains—
you're not so secret

something in the little blade of grass
tree leaf shivering
something wasted remains

perhaps it is only an echo of your breath
comes back to you,
but no request
goes unheard

The Mathematics of Talking about Love

returns to a pile of dry leaves

every reason you have for every expression
of love, every plan you carefully craft
or bluster together
balls up into
a pile of dry leaves—
your first joyous moment

remember your first
joyous moment
and give that
to your love

Don't Fear the Easy Path

simply because it is easy—

all other paths being equal,
the easiest path is best

but be aware that ease
is often a shortcut
to where you've begun

you could tread water
in the shallows
all your life

and never try for
the island on the horizon

Every Broken Little Thing

As my children grew older,
some fear grew larger within me.
I wrote poems to warn them
about the dark parts of life, the power
of long memories and regret.
I wanted to teach them how to collect light,
but I was only teaching them how to
hide from darkness, how to live my life
only better than I had lived it.
I was afraid that one day I would look
at them and see my brother and me, that they
would somehow become my brother and me,
        and that would make me the father.

A great poet once said to recall
your first joyous moment
and give that to your love,
so to my love I give the day we met.
But once when I was very small
and our house full of cigarette smoke,
light creased golden like an angel's wing
through living room curtains
and I heard a tap at the window
and ran excited outside to see the sun
but instead found a bird, broken and tangled
in a rosebush beneath the window.

I stood watching it for long minutes,
wanting to help, to make it unbroken
but there was nothing I could do.
Was this my first real joy—
a first shocking taste of balance?
How life and love twist and churn
with death and pain? That life is harsh
and beauty ever-present?
That romance and reality, like tide waters
ebb and flow, and that they must?
        The bird was tiny,
          the rosebush wild.

And so in a world of harsh balance
whole philosophies arise, unintelligible to me then
because I read them all in a language of depression and
depression is a language of babble that hurts to speak.
I had thought of love as a real thing and the heart
imaginary—all I've ever taught my children is how
to find kindness in a brutal world. That you can't arm
yourself with love. That joy is never a weapon. And that
I admit I'm ashamed to talk of pain and so, instead,
I relive it over and over in my head and over and over
in what I see ahead for my children until finally I break
and sing that hollow song everyone knows in the dark.

And so I look for ways to make myself feel happy but
there is no single button to push or simple pill to take.
And the truth is that drugs work.
Xanax will make you feel good
and alcohol makes your pain go away.

And they do.
> But not for long enough.

And when that good feeling leaves you, which it will,
it always takes a greater piece than it gave,
and it keeps taking and taking and taking until
you've wasted yourself down to some exquisite nothingness
slouched against the kitchen wall mumbling into your chest,
> *Well, at least I'm happy.*

Depression is a language of babble that hurts to speak
and still I read the world and translate as best I can,
but now I know how to teach my children that love
isn't all you need, but that there's no life without it.
That life is a sunbeam, and love,
a broken bird in a rosebush—
and that every broken little thing in life
is still a miracle we must not let go of.

Breakthrough

In my work, my gloves wear through,
revealing skin, knuckles, fingernails
worn tough by this regular grind.
Always the first to break through
is my wedding ring, which looks
at first sight, like
a golden worm,
cresting the surface
of rich garden earth after a rain,

or the first streak of morning
cracking the darkness of night.

This comforts me while I work,
when the drear overtakes the mind,
any thought you've once had blanches
and that old stiffness rises and plateaus
and fingers shudder and want to quit
and callus (mercifully achieved) splits,
opening a seam of deep pink,
the rebirth of pain once overcome.

Seeing the ring, I remember why I work—
the ring not being my wife, herself
(my wife much more brilliant, though
just as scuffed from work of her own)
but something to keep with me, to catch

my eye at an odd glance with a glimmer,
to elicit a smile I forgot I had.

I'm not worried about my wedding ring
getting scuffed up, not really,
this soft metal with the steel that abrades it—
after all the ring is just a ring.
And what it
signifies, what it
proves day in day out
is much, much stronger than steel.

Adjustments

At the Jeep plant today,
from across the commissary, I saw
Becky Lautner (that's not her real name)
hook her two rough thumbs
through the fabric of her Iron Maiden t-shirt
deep into some recess of her brassiere,
and with a slight wince and a sort of
swooping grace hoist her two, frankly massive
breasts into a more comfortable, or maybe
just a less uncomfortable position.
                And if that's not enough
already to spark notice, she then
heaved out such a cathartic sigh of relief
that even I felt it from all the way across this
vast field of laminate tabletops and Bakelite
lunch trays, and it made me instantly, and
hopefully forgivably, feel a little guilty
for complaining about my aching feet.

Gap in the Line!

Gap in the line!
Gap in the line!

Everybody quick!
Scurry to your phones!
We may only have seconds!

Check your Facebooks and Twitters.
Gap in the line, fellas!

You!
Poor guy with flip phone
scurry to your cellophane sleeve
of butter crackers tucked amongst
the crate full of gaskets—
now is your moment!
Drink your water and
Lick your lips!

Gap in the line!
Looks like a big one!

Old timers!
Shamble to your fold-out chairs
and Igloo coolers.
Take a nip off that tit
and tuck it back away.

Scan the line for another old timer...
knowingly nod, and
check your smokes.

There's a gap in the line!
Could start up any second!

You! Douchebag greasy muscle bound
twenty something.
Now's your time to make your move!
Peacock yourself
to the cute girls, next line over—
here's your chance!
You know they watch you
as you hoist and rivet.

Gap in the line!
It's the blue light special!
Could break anytime!

You, especially,
18-year-old legacy boy.
You get it hardest.
Stretch your shoulders now
and flex your knees.
Pump your hands to prepare
for what's coming.
Tape up your fingers and make your
Papa proud.

Fugue

She tells me I shouldn't live in the past, but
her television is playing reruns of The Price Is Right.
I say
> *those who forget the past*
> *are doomed to repeat it,*

but I know what she meant—
I'm just being belligerent.
She's fantasizing about fabulous prizes
while I've been telling stories again,
about boyhood, about country life, nostalgia
and all sorts of fuzzy fiction I refresh
like a playwright, telling it my way.

My memories are all fictions anyway,
memories collected over past presents, rewritten,
redemptions unattained at the time
regained upon revision and re-creation.
Like the day that dog chased me and my bike
down the one long hill on County Road 1570.
        Dog? There were probably four of them.
Vicious. Single-minded.
Vivaldi Adagio fills the air, time slows.
Witness the calf muscle strain, the pedals
punished under sneaker by sheer force of effort.
Go, little man, go!

Or the time Ricky Crites stopped by
with a new aluminum baseball bat. And

twelve other friends. I played outfield
with no glove. Gutsy move. A swing of the bat
and the ball arcs so high it becomes a distant speck.
And in sound the horns, deep and resonant
as I begin my run to catch it.
          Hang on. Go back. I love this part.
And in sound the horns, deep and resonant
as I begin my run to catch it.
The eyes are focused,
bead of sweat on forehead.
There's no way. There's no way.
The horns rise and crescendo, the body stretched
level to the ground, the arm, the hand,
the ball, will he make it?
Yes! By God, yes! Before our very eyes.
A bare-handed catch to end the game!
The crowd goes mad with excitement.
The walls may fall.
Ladies and gentlemen, remember this day!

There was no catch. I made that up.
No crowd. No horns. No friends.
No one went mad with excitement—
          we didn't even play ball.
Ricky got a sweet bat though.
We spent half an hour hitting driveway gravel
into the front yard, just to hear the ting.
But I like my version better.

My memories are all fictions anyway,
and there's nothing wrong with fiction.

Maybe next time there'll be six dogs.
Dobermans. Accompanied by a brisk fugue.
Heavy bass. Lots of tension.
Yes, that'll do it.
And all of it in full color.

Background Files

In high school, a friend named Jim Barr
had the nickname of Kareem, but I didn't know why.
He played basketball, sure, but he wasn't very good.
And beyond that he was a short, blonde, white boy
from the country in Ohio— in no way was he Kareem.

Thirty years later, quite out of the blue,
for no good reason I could tell, it hit me. I got it.
The nickname— *Kareem Abdul Jim Barr.*
Ok. All right. I laughed at first, but then anger. Fury!

How many grocery bags have been left at check-out counters?
How many mugs of coffee spilt from the roof of my car?
How many keys misplaced?
Rooms entered with no idea what I came in for?

But you're telling me, all the while, somewhere
in the background, my mind is *still* working
on that goddam Jim Barr nickname?

Tell me, how many more mental hamsters
have given their lives spinning in their wheels
searching for solutions to other worthless mysteries?

I need a reset button for my brain. Something to purge
those background files running recursive scripts,
seeking answers to adolescent questions
when I have plenty to keep in mind today.

The roast comes out of the oven at six,
tomorrow is trash day, and for Christ's sake
let the dog back in. It's cold outside.

In Fire Times

In fire times
it's important to remember
to stay low— don't breathe!
unless you have a mask or cloth
to cover your face.
Breathe through those
but nothing else.

In fire times
remember to speak up
yell if you need to—
the roar of the flames
will try to match you,
smoke will choke you.
If you're to be heard,
call it all out!

In fire times
everyone will leave you behind—
they will go without you
of course they will, believe it!
No one will be there for you
but there you'll be
alone, remembering to stay low,
trying to yell and not breathe.

And just before the fire
swallows you up anyway
licking your sweet neck
biting at every part of you,
in your very last moment
your final thought will be
just how absurd
you'll look burnt naked,
an eternal smile of skull and teeth.

Lori Listening to Sarah Vaughan

I believed you just then, if never before,
your eyes closing to the music. With our
awkward whirlwind fitting two broken lives
somehow together, with whatever unlikely love

evolves into perfect real friendship,
I believed you when you closed your eyes
just then. Just then a certainty, the look on your face
somewhere between ecstasy and peace,

comfort and seduction, I saw that unguarded moment.
All these things wrong with the world whispered away
for some long second. All the fears and hunger
gone away like morning mist to the sun.

Our young, long histories banging together. I saw
through your lies, of course I did, and lied myself.
But just then, music around you, all these things right
with the world, a deep sigh, a sip of black coffee.

Soirée

When the night finally takes me, and I truckle
off to sleep, my conscience pulls on a robe,
creeps downstairs and paces the living room,
tugging at his beard in nervous bursts.

The child of my memory slumps to the basement
to the unused coal room, musty and cobwebbed,
and sits in the dark corner, knees to chin,
thinking long and hard about what it is he's done.

The husband and father in me checks the locks
once more, peeks into quiet bedrooms, turns
the thermostat down one reasonable degree,
looks to see if tomorrow the lawn needs mowed.

My daily fear skitters through the house, flinching
at each floorboard creak, drip of faucet, sure to
duck past the hallway mirror, avoiding the vanity,
trembling in the infinity between bathroom mirrors.

But my joyfulness will have none of that— sneaks
a cigarette from the pantry shelf behind the canned beets,
puts on a favorite jazz record and dances in the dark
until dawn light creeps upon bedroom window sill.

This is why, I know, some days upon waking
I rise and scratch and groan my way to the kitchen,
swirl the remains of yesterday's coffee pot,
even more tired than when I laid down to sleep.

While Leaves Fall in Autumn

The old Japanese maple in our back yard
spills red out of its leaves like juice
bursting from an overripe berry,

like a volcanic lava plume so radiant
that when golden hour sun hits the tree
our white house glows a deep pink.

And though the leaves fall fast, cover our
yard and garden in a stunning blanket to make way
for coming spring buds, they still glow like coals

smoldering even as snow falls. So,
why is it that in this, the autumn of my life,
my skin grows only paler, my beard greyer?

No dropping of bright leaves to rake and pile,
but only slow shedding into paltry wet hairballs
after-shower in the bathroom trash?

Our maple tree slips off its cardinal camisole in
an unwittingly lush display, and reminds me
that my winter will have no spring.

Where is my lava plume before white ash,
my shocking eruption before the fade— where is
the burst of bright before my dead end?

Love Poems

The best love poems don't start out
as love poems. They start out as
regular, ordinary things— like dish soap,
being late for work, things that wriggle
in earth, or changing a car tire.

You start writing, just doodles at first,
playing with words, looking for patterns,
when suddenly there she is—
it's your wife in September. And the things
that wriggle in earth begin to take shape,

the car tire lines itself up somehow
to mean something else, and out of
the blue you've written a love poem
and you don't know how. Not really.
Like love, sometimes it just comes to you.

Ode to Our Blue Curtain

We put up a thrift store curtain
in our kitchen window, but
the rest of our kitchen is still terrible.
Vinyl floor tiles cracked at corners and beyond,
electric wall-plates suspect,
plaster tectonically shifting—
the drop ceiling is half dropped-out.

Our blue curtain conceals:
a bud vase crucifying a desiccated avocado pit,
thumbnail-clipped toothpicks propping it up,
a small palmful of some kind of seed
(probably greens) dried beyond usefulness,
and a pendant my daughter said she lost
a blue glass dolphin in a triumphant arc.

Our blue curtain, should it be laid flat,
would still wear the sun-bleached stripes
of its former home— those woeful, faded
blues and not-so-blues, so sad,
soft lines hard-worn,
overlooked, forgotten.

But our blue curtain also conceals
our great joy in this woeful kitchen.
The making of food, the congregation of people,
the lingering conversations, and the patient
tending of things to be shared.

Our blue curtain is a happy sham.
It is just right— It runs the length
of what is visible looking in
and it has a pretty ruffle.

Our blue curtain cost us 50¢
from the Salvation Army
and now we can cook eggs naked
without a care in the world.

The Best Poets I Know Are Workers

I admit my bias toward working people—
I pull more wisdom from a bead of sweat
creasing down a dusty brow
than I do from the wild hair of the ascetic
tweed jacket elbow patches and blear eyes.

Something there is nourishing about pushing
hands into soil. Fingers like roots seeking
connection and synthesis.

And what is a poet if not a farmer of truth—
like a seed, a truth will grow
where it is dropped on paper,
will take root.

There is an alchemy to poetry
that farmers know,
that factory workers live,
that those in Tyvek suits
shimmying flashlight-in-mouth
through dank crawlspaces understand.

There is an alchemy to poetry
that workers know even if
they don't know they know it.

I admit my bias toward working people,
the raw but rich over the academic,
my jealousy toward Neruda's odes
to common things. I write my odes
to socks in my workboots each day.

I admit my bias toward working people—
I see how they make barren soil fertile, how
they cultivate and create. And I too want
my fingers to root, I want to drop my ink
seeds and tell the beautiful truth.

The Bumblebee and the Falcon

There is flight and then there's flight,
there is a bumblebee and there is a falcon.

In college, one professor says, *There is no reality.*
Another professor says, *There are infinite realities.*
They are both teaching me.

I want to lock them together in a room
full of philosophy and physics texts
and let them battle to the death.

Only, I know that the death match will end
and when the victory door opens
a poet will step out and tell me
something I'm not ready to hear.

So, which is the answer? I'll ask.
He will reply, *It is ok to be conflicted.*

My pen buzzes like a bumblebee in my grasp,
but some days I write like a falcon flies.

Force of Habit

before he placed the pistol
to his temple
and depressed the trigger

he first took off his glasses
out of sheer force of habit
and folded them into their case

which he closed up tight
and patted twice with his hand

safe and sound
safe and sound

The Barcode on Your Head

This is not another poem about
the corporate consumption of humanity.
This is no Orwellian dystopia
with barcodes on heads
for easier access to bodies and minds.
This is just a poem about a shower.

Less about a shower, I guess,
this is a poem about growing old.
Well, not so much about growing old, but rather
having grown old without realizing it.
This is a poem about stepping out of the shower
one morning before work, thinking about coffee
while you wipe steam from the bathroom mirror,
only to find a distinct, undeniable barcode
broadly printed across the top of your head.
This is a poem about the barcode on your head.

You stand, motionless
while steam overtakes the mirror
afraid to wipe it clear again, but then once re-wiped
there's that barcode of sparse hairs desperately
clinging together, laying in lines thick and thin
with bright white scalp beneath.
This is a poem about the barcode
you didn't know was on your head.
You touch your finger to the mirror
just to make sure it's real.

You watch, dumbfounded
as steam slowly softens the image until you
are just a foggy silhouette. No more barcode.
Would you look at that— you could be twenty.
This is just a poem about not wiping
your bathroom mirror after a shower.

Two Birds

The assembly line is a monster that is always hungry
and you feed it all day long
for thirty plus years, if you're lucky.
Cycles of forty seconds, twelve hours a day
for most of your adult life,
it's important to point at something specific
in the blur that is the last week
or month, and to give it a name
and to make it mean something.
So complaining becomes a pastime—
everyone here has the toughest job in the factory.

The assembly line is a monster that is always hungry
and as the years pass you complain and complain,
and your back begins to hunch and your legs begin to bow,
and your hands slowly distort to better fit your tools.
You sometimes quietly pray for a breakdown somewhere
to stop the line, even just for a minute—
and when it finally happens you look at each other
and you say *free money, I'll take it,*
and you say *any downtime is good time,*
then you drink your water and rub fists into your back.

The assembly line is a monster that is always hungry
until it isn't—
until the economy dips
and the company decides to ship some jobs overseas,

but, you know, not too many,
and they'll only close one plant each
in Illinois, Indiana, Ohio.
But it's your plant that closes,
and so now you're trying to decide
whether any downtime is actually good time,
and your buddy at the stamping plant down the street
says you should've expected this and planned better,
God knows he has.

Now you and six thousand other workers spend your days
making what money you can, and your nights are restless
with hard hands rubbing the back of your sweaty neck,
and what sleep you get are just dreams of getting back
into the plant that you hoped to get out of.
The days still blur by, but now each day is a new worry,
a new grind to see if work's available anywhere,
what you can get, for how long,
what's the pay, and is it worth it?
You know you'll take the job even if it isn't.

There is no more monster to feed
until one day there is, and isn't it great
they're opening the factory back up?
But by now you're so beat down
you don't really believe it anyway
until the power plant starts buzzing back
and the smokestacks start belching grey steam
and the waste water slough starts to froth
and you get that call from your steward—
are you still around?
You are.

You go through the gate and head toward your station
and you find that you've only been back for thirty
    seconds, but
you already feel like you wish it were quitting time,
and everyone walking the corridor with you is
    bowlegged,
with Igloo coolers and gallons of water from Kroger.
The whole building is humming,
but it matches the humming of your bones,
and you suddenly realize that you're not just hungry
but hungry for the noise and heat and grease
and the calluses that will split and that you will filthily
    suck at
at the line breaks you silently pray for.

You walk past a wall of welder transformers
which makes you think back to the day
two little birds flew into the body shop
and couldn't figure out how to get out—
how one of them just hid away up in the trusses
(and even stayed around for months afterward,
occasionally pecking food from dumpsters
and sometimes shitting on the boss's desk,
which made it an honorary union member
as far as you're concerned),

but the other bird panicked
and madly darted back and forth and back and forth
while the workers all chuckled and pointed
because if that idiot bird would just
fly out of the dock bay door he'd be free.

And we smiled and we called him bird-brain
until he slammed into the heavy steel cage wall
by those transformers and momentarily stunned himself—
and suddenly it's not so funny as we all realize together
that little fellow is going to kill himself.

So now there's a phalanx of union workers
with long-handled push-brooms held high
and beer bellies blobbing from beneath tee shirts,
trying to guide the tiny bird out of the dock door
like fat awkward cattlemen wrangling a frantic calf.
And there's a good moment there when we all think it's working
until it flies high, fast, suddenly plonking beak-first
into a second story window
and tumbles down to the floor so softly
that when it strikes the cement
it doesn't even make a sound.

The push-brooms lower,
and we all look for a few moments
until someone sweeps the body
out of the door and off the dock.

The sudden memory of those two little birds
is still buzzing in your mind as you finally get back
to your station that seems to have been
patiently waiting for you all those months.
And it strikes you then that you've worked with people like that—
who had those panicked eyes and shaky hands
and steamed-up safety glasses, who missed their rivets

just because they were afraid they were going to,
and no matter what you say to them
they can not shake that feeling
until one day they just walk out of the factory
and never come back. But then it hits you just as hard
that that makes you the other bird,
the one that's still trapped but doesn't seem to mind.

And you wonder, as you line up your tools and check your stock,
which bird you'd rather be.
But your air pressure's good and the bell sounds,
so you just depress the safety button
and fire seven steel rivets into the fender bar
smoothly dead center—
three in the middle, two on each side
three in the middle, two on each side
three in the middle, two on each side.

Keeper of the Loaves

for John Swaile

As we till and hoe our garden, grateful
the frost has passed, it's well into springtime
and we're late to plant as usual.

We've planned the planting, prepared
the soil. We imagine the harvest. We work
our bodies hard to make up for misspent time.

We are smiling our way toward exhaustion—
toil and sweat, a little more work
and then we'll rest.

Earlier my wife baked bread
and I can smell it from the garden.

I say to her something our friend used to say,
The Lord is the keeper of the loaves.

I say, *Honey, you are the keeper of the loaves!*
and suddenly it hits me that John is gone.

I wipe sweat from my naked face.
Ten years now, John is gone.

All these years and still gone.

Horses and Art in the Age of COVID-19

Yes, it is true that horses
don't paint the roan canvas
of their flesh. And yes

wheat fields were here
long before Van Gogh
picked up his horse hair brush,

wild horses and wooly bison grazed
tall grass long before first artistic humans
stick-figured them dumb on cave walls.

Yet here we are today fighting
amongst ourselves as a virus
drowns us out, gasping one by one

and here I still am sheltering in place,
nervously painting portraits of smiling
faces onto wood panels—

smiling faces which can't weep for lost
daughters or gasp for air, painted faces that
could never trade family ties for tribal lies.

Yes, I know we rise each time we fall, but oh
how we fall back each time we rise.
Just think how in the many years

before cave walls
first tasted the sacred ink
of humanity's potential

horses had
already perfected
being horses.

To Rhyme a Poem
a rondeau

To rhyme a poem and not make it sound
like you're rhyming, consider some profound
truth— then write your lines in rhyme! If you don't
perfectly rhyme the words, then try a slant
(even though it's not perfect, write it down).

Enjambment will help not to make every rhyme-sound
fall at the ends of lines. Wrap them around
so it's not obvious the rhymes are there, if you want
to rhyme a poem

without it sounding forced. After you've wound
your lines so the rhymes are hidden, I've found
it's best, in successful poems, to try to plant
some other little trick, something clever. I can't
really say more— but know that artful ways abound
to rhyme a poem.

Two Drunken Poems Composed by a Tree

this is a good poem
because this is my poem
this is the poem I thought up today
tuesday october 5:05pm, sitting by my tree
this is this:
    what I think
    and what comes from me
and that's real good I think
because I think I think real good
(I know my grammar isn't real good
but still this is what I think
when I think real good
and that's real good I think)

***

I won't write a poem today
because I'm drunk
and not in much of a state
to write
I would rather sleep than write
right now
so that's what I'll do
(sleep, not write)
good night

This Is not a Pipe
for Rob
after "The Treachery of Images," by René Magritte

Sugar maples drop their whirligigs through cool
autumn breeze as we choose the perfect words to inscribe
on your gravestone. Cancer, discovered too late,
and months to prepare— so we are thoughtful.
These are the perfect words, we decide.

The words on paper are lovely, but they
are not real things. The words on paper
know their place in philosophy. Your cheekbones
push through your skin like little pink crabapples. That
is what is real. Your gravestone will be polished granite.

Now I trace my finger on polished granite, along
the height of the letter B of Born September 6, 1972.
It is almost one year since we chose those words,
and now that I touch them in stone, I see our mistake.
Ceci n'est pas une pipe. This thing I see is not real.

Epitaphs, even the perfect words, are empty, lonely things.
Our childhood fistfights were real. Our euchre games,
backyard football, nervous questions about girls, those were real.
Our time together was real, but these lovely words were better
when we spoke them together. On stone they disappear.

Your grave rests next to a stand of elm trees,
seeds falling onto granite slabs like tiddlywinks
and I swipe them away with a rough hand.
There is no reason to read your epitaph—
instead I remember the day we chose it.

And I watch elm seeds curl through the breeze of
another year's autumn, and think of how those seedlings
will rise up hopeful next spring, like little fingers poking up
through thin blades of grass, only to be lopped off when
the caretaker comes to prepare the grounds for new mourners.

Dr. Don Bop
a memory from a reading at Calvinos
Toledo, Ohio 2012

Few poets I've known
so enjoyable to hear,
even when I had no idea
what they were talking about.

It's like his head was
a train track switching station
with poems flying down those lines...
and he's busy bopping
back and forth between them,
hooting and shouting
whispering and dancing.

Spontaneous poetry,
jazz poems,
words and words and singing those words

and a table full of scattered papers and
  Oh! I've dropped my poem
no matter
how about this one?

Never missing a beat, but maybe once
to realize he doesn't remember
which point he had started

and then he smacks a table top,
with a flat hand and slips
into a three-second-long salsa dance
(with a suspicious grin)
while he grabs for another paper
        and reads it,
realizing just then
it was only a receipt
from a service station,

and so he reads it,
and man,
it sounds great.

Why I Write Poetry

I write poetry because I spent eight years
learning how to be a scientist,
and I couldn't stand it anymore

I write poetry because when I see a blank sheet of paper,
I want to fill it

I write poetry because sometimes I read so much
my head gets full

I write poetry because you can find
ten thousand poems about the moon,
but I wanted ten thousand and one

****

I write poetry because everything
hasn't been said quite yet

I write poetry because when I talk to myself,
people think I'm crazy— but if I write it down,
they think I'm talented

I write poetry because when words fall out of my hands,
they need a place to rest

****

I write poetry because
these haggard factory hands can do more
than just build Jeeps

I write poetry because
America puts brown children in cages

I write poetry because
America has always put brown children in cages
and we keep saying *this is not who we are*

****

I write poetry because
a society that cannot produce poets is a dead society

I write poetry because
I want to resurrect my father

I write poetry because
my father has no grave,
so my poems are his constant tombs

****

I write poetry because Mr. Whitmore told me
he liked the poem I showed him in high school

I write poetry because
I bullshit myself through most days,
but I believe myself when I write

I write poetry because I use an antique typewriter
that stops me from rebvising as I type

****

I write poetry because my photo albums are full,
but I still have some notebooks

I write poetry because sometimes a tree is just a tree,
but of course not… it is always more

I write poetry because anyone can write a poem,
but not just anyone will be a poet

****

I write poetry because some of the best people
I know are poets

I write poetry because some of the worst people
I know are poets

I write poetry because
John Swaile told me to

****

I write poetry because free speech is a miracle
that can be killed by the same people
who decree that corporations are people
and money is speech

I write poetry because
poetry kills fascists

I write poetry because
poems are beacons and this world can be dark

I write poetry because Jeremy Kaiser beat me up
in the eighth grade and said, *Poetry is gay*
And now Jeremy Kaiser is in a poem

****

I write poetry because I don't like to talk very much,
but I have a lot to say

I write poetry because
poetry is big medicine for a disjointed mind

I write poetry because this country is belching
fire upon a tinderbox world, and Tom Barden tells me
you do not have the right to remain silent

****

I write poetry because I'm too shy to sing

I write poetry because I can't give birth

I write poetry because you can only put
so many words on your tombstone,
so you've got to make them count

Athanor

ekphrastic poem after the painting
Athanor, by Anselm Kiefer

this is a good fire we burn
the very heat of which purifies,
nourishes. and who would refuse
the diamonds our ashes will become

fire brings us closer to
spiritual perfection—
a secret fire, alchemical, burns
for generations, purifies generations,

generates purity in its self-feeding furnace.
bread ovens nourish bodies with fire,
the architecture of our bodies burned
heavenward, ashes to ashes

and who would refuse the diamonds
our ashes will become—   the gold
culled from the soil of our bodies.
who would refuse to make us great again—

think of all the gilt halls, houses gilt,
a gilt regime of a world on fire
purifying our many bodies—
the world is on fire

and who would refuse perfection—
the furnaces purify, they perfect.
to enter the kingdom of heaven
we must transform— our skin

become spirit. we are conceived
as purity of spirit. a greatness,
an ideal— and who would refuse
to make our bodies great again

all our paths like rail lines
lead to the bread ovens
this is a good fire we burn
this is a good fire we burn

the world is on fire
all our bodies, gilt
the world is on fire
ashes to ashes

I Remember

a poem for the Remembrance Sunday

She passed away thirty five years ago
and I can't remember what she looked like—
        my wife, and I can't remember her face.
I remember things in flashes, feelings,
I remember the War.
I remember the end, shot four times
        and I laid there panting like an animal—
        waiting, freezing, on German ice.
I remember being grabbed by the collar
        and dragged to safety
        by a medic I never knew.
I remember looking beside me,
        the body of my brother dragged along with me—
I can't remember his name,
        not even on a day like that
        but I remember his jaw frozen open,
        his fingers still curled around his revolver,
and I remember that smoke floated from his chest
        like a snake.

I don't remember being sent home, but
I remember coming home to her—
I remember that feeling.
I remember we had four years together,
        and children, two children.

I remember—
        I remember when they were born.
I remember being young with her, and
I remember when she died.
I found her in our bed,
        curled with her knees tucked to her chest.
I can remember the night before,
I remember that we made love that night before,
        and laid, watching each other
        for hours after.
I remember it seemed like hours.
I don't remember her face,
        not even on nights like those,
        but I remember how I felt,
        and I remember sharing a cigarette with her,
and I remember that the smoke floated from her lips
        like a prayer.

A Trip to the Zoo

It's ninety degrees and sticky humid
and she is pushing her three-year-old toddler
in a stroller, her five-year-old son alongside.
He is asking for a snack that she doesn't have.
When she tells him there is no snack, he says
but I just want it. And she explains over and over that
there is no snack to have. She's not keeping one for herself,
there is no snack. She doesn't have one. The snack is gone.
But he insists and she is losing patience.
Each time they roll past a Pepsi vendor or
lemon ice stand, the toddler's hands spring forth
from the stroller, fingers flexing, clutching, pulsing,
grabbing at, grabbing for, begging, crying, repeating *I want.*
I want. I want. I want. I want. I want. I want.

In thirty-six hours she will be in a corporate boardroom
filled with a group of middle management men
having basically the same conversation.
They will ask for something, and when they're informed
that that something doesn't exist, they will just
ask for it again. She will keep her patience
lightly beneath her skin, and point out, again,
sometimes using spreadsheets and charts,
why, again, the nonexistent is nonexistent.

Before the long walk back to the van
where she will pack up the stroller and bags,

the sleeping toddler and cranky son, she stops
pauses before the exotic bird enclosure to watch
the colorful birds brightly flitting back
and forth and back again, branch to branch,
carefree and unburdened by the world outside,
every day within their four glass walls,
every day beneath their broad glass ceiling.

Love Is Something Like Hot Sauce

I'm not saying that hot sauce is love
or that hot sauce is the meaning of life—
what I'm saying is we make certain promises
to each other, and then fate takes over.

It's like at our wedding when we stood
together beneath that giant oak tree
and it was beautiful and symbolic
and I heard a noise and looked up
and an acorn hit me on the head.
It's like that is what I'm saying.

Or it's like how even though it's not your job
to mow the yard, you still secretly
envy the pride I take over freshly-cut clover.
And, yes, I know you would mow
our sad, little clover-yard if I were gone,
but I'm not. We're in this together.

And it's like that time at the hospital
with the emergency C-section
and Scott had an Apgar score of 2
and we looked at each other—
     do you remember how we looked
at each other when we realized that
life and death were both present
and that we needed to be together,
and it was both terrifying and serene?
It's like that, too.

Or it's like how when I do the dishes it's always
in the afternoon and that drives you bonkers
because when you do the dishes it's
early in the morning, which leaves you, as you say,
the entire rest of the day to do— a lot, to be honest.
But not mowing our sad, little clover-yard.
That's for sure.

But maybe it's mostly like when you
get me a little something just because I
had a rough day, and I come home from work to find
hot sauce— and it's the good kind of hot sauce I like,
only usually it's too expensive to justify buying,
so it was probably on sale, but either way
you saw it and thought of me and so there it is,
and truthfully it isn't about hot sauce at all—

What I'm saying is this:
we may not know what fate will throw at us
but we know just the ways
to make each other happy.
Love is like that.

Myole Corona

Iused to love my ole Corona and
then I got angrywith a thought
ans I punched itskeys and
now its broked and
it dont wanto let
mesaywhat
iwant it
tosay
.

The Bird Shit Cleaners

The bird shit cleaners rise each day
in their Genie boom lifts to scrape
bird shit from the head and shoulders,
the face and hands of Robert E. Lee
astride his muscled regal stallion
as rock pigeons and laughing gulls
continue to release their
cloacal payloads like judgements
upon the very face of power.

Why? Why do the bird shit cleaners
wake so early each morning to wield
their putty knives and polyfiber brushes
to uncake and defecalate these monuments,
stone and bronze testaments preserving
the myths of preternatural conquerors
who have long since succumbed
to what nature always demands?
What has Stonewall Jackson done

for you lately? Or ever?
Is this some type of Stockholm servitude,
festooned with the scars of former lashings
borne blood-deep into the genes of workers?
Or have they simply been tempted into serving
a more indifferent conqueror? The mighty dollar
supplanting the once-mighty confederate general.

Has the allure of slightly-above-minimum-wage pay
and 80/20 healthcare with $2,000 deductibles
achieved that which the great achievers
could never have foreseen?

Are the bird shit cleaners, then, servants
of the bosses or servants of the birds?
Servants of the cormorants?
Of swarms of gulls?
With each chalky-white donation
that dribbles from the mustached lips
and bearded chin of J.E.B. Stuart,
the common domestic pigeon has done
more real work for the bird shit cleaning economy
than all congresspeople and job-creators combined.

Rise, then! Rise bird shit cleaners!
Rise up! Decline your boom lifts and
recline your ladders. Bucket your brushes
into the fetid waters of failed insurrection.
Your hands were granted to you to hold
other hands, not the lash handles
of the shadows of long-gone masters.
With leverage all monuments will fall.
Or, just let them stand where they stand
and collect the full compliment
of what their memory has earned.

Family Secrets

You might ask me to reveal all our secrets
things that happened in the dark
things I've heard through walls—
or stories I don't know to be true
but how the air thickens
at the offhand mention of a name,
and the whole family suddenly becomes
weird robots discussing potluck recipes—

If you want me to reveal all our secrets
you must first snuff me out, dead
and gone. Burn my body long
until all that remains is
soft white ash, brittle black bone.
Let an Ohio breeze draw my dust
across a cornfield, then you may sift
through my bones— see if they tell you a thing.

After Reading Ted Kooser All Night at Work

I hold in my two large hands a tin box
full of colored pencils— good ones
given as a present— and a sketch pad
of stout textured white paper,
and realize that in the proper hands
this is all that is necessary to produce
a masterpiece.

My hands are clumsy mitts, I know, thick
and a little shaky. Who would blame Picasso
for being talented? Francis Bacon, van Gogh,
Matisse? It never crosses my mind to expect
that of myself. Yet I scritch and scratch
my pencils, sip my tea, and happily sigh.

And so it is, after reading Ted Kooser
I sit on break at work with my notebook and pen,
or at home before my little Remington 5
and a fresh sheet of typing paper, in the early
morning after-shift hush to write.

Did you know that the words Ted Kooser uses
are the very same words I use? The same paper,
same pen, same tin box of words. So I smile and sigh,
listen to the words in my head, let my mind wander.

And then I turn myself around, sip my tea,
and go happily back to my typing.

Lady on the Condom Machine

On an old, worn, white metal box on the wall
in the bathroom of a small club in west Toledo—
a cowgirl on the label of a condom machine.

Picture the scene: crimson chaps, silver fringe
with matching Stetson and boots— topless,
as all rugged cowgirls must be, tasseled pasties
discreetly covering the nipples of teardrop breasts
the exact shape of youth.

Her skin is flawless and smooth, creamy white
flushed with pink, but ink has faded through decades
leaving an overall hue of chartreuse
blushing toward turquoise.

She holds a six-shooter erect, which appears
too large for her slight hand, as her lips freeze
pursed to blow? have blown? gunsmoke from the tip.

A twinkle in her eye, but has it been airbrushed
for effect? Or is this the sparkle-flash of some slick agent
coercing fresh, new talent into the studio—
covergirl promises of full-page spreads?
Did she know what she was getting into?
Did she think it exciting? Did she know?

Either way she seems self-assured,
and we lock eyes at the urinal as I'm
in a particularly vulnerable moment.
But with that seductive look on her face
you know exactly what she wants. She wants you
to put a quarter in the machine.
Or perhaps fifty cents if you're a gentleman
more concerned with her pleasure.

She can't be more than twenty years old there.
If she has weathered the storms of life,
God willing and the deductibles don't rise,
today she's someone's Busia or
or Nana or Yiayia sending cards
with crisp five dollar bills on birthdays
even to her fifty-year-old children.

And she never misses a holiday card
to all of the grand and step-grandchildren.
They know the smell of her house—
it's a nice little house with petunias in front,
the bowl of scented fabric flower petals
on bath stand, line of porcelain elves
along the kitchen window sill.

Everyone in the neighborhood knows the rasp
of her voice, the firmness of her hugs,
how she whistles in her spring garden.
Birds know her feeders all winter,
with extra sunflower seeds for cardinals,
and a flat-palm slap on the window for blue jays.

Picture the scene: crimson chaps, silver fringe
with matching Stetson and boots— tucked beneath
warm afghans and soft bed linens, nestled
next to a tied bundle of letters
in the stout cedar chest at the foot of a bed
in the bedroom of a nice little house
in west Toledo.

Perfection

I wrote a song one day.
It was only one note long
but it was perfect.
I played it over and over and over.
And every time someone asked me why
my song was only one note long,
I just lied and lied and lied.

I'd say things like,
        my song is being ironic,
            or, Beethoven's first was short too.
I'd say, it's a concentrated single jazz bop,
        or, it's the beat of the heart,
        an echo of the Big Bang.

I'd say, I ran out of paper and so I had to
        write my song on a grain of rice.
I'd say, it's post-pre-post-modern, and hope
        they don't know that that means nothing.

I'd say, this is the sound my heart makes when it breaks,
        the piano I compose on only has one key,
            it would've been longer but I was interrupted
by a man from Porlock,

I'd say, this is what it sounds like when doves cry,
        sometimes less is more,
            try to listen to the notes I'm not playing.

But the truth is, if I'm being honest,
(and this is just between you and me)
the song would've been longer, but
I wrote down that first note and it was perfect.

And if I've learned one thing in this world
it's that you just don't mess with perfection.

I Can Feel It
for Stormi
for the reopening of poetry at The Trunk

A physical heart has only
so many beats to beat—
only so many beats left in it—
A hard truth that we all know, and
just fold our hands and pray to keep goin'.
A physical heart that beat its last beat
and sparked a collective gasp
a wish for peaceful rest
across the Midwest
one summer morning—
a collective gasp heard sweeping
from Chicago to Toledo
from the 2nd City to the Glass city—
A collective gasp of shock for that last
beat
we all knew might come, but
still shocked us when we heard,
caught us off-guard
when we got that final word.
A collective sigh of loss,
of sudden sadness,
of heads bowed low
for that one last beat,
a final beat.

Paula, who I knew better here as Stormi—
Stormi with an i—
whose heart not long ago
beat its last beat, but we all know
that's not true.
She might not be standing up here with me now,
but she's here with us.
I can feel it.
And her heart still beats—
I can feel it.
Stormi's heart still beats in the streets of Chicago—
her heart still beats in these streets of Toledo—
her heart still beats in the bodies and souls
of her sons— a Queen's princes—
in the way she talked, in her confident walk,
in the way she dressed, a feast for the senses.
Her heart still beats in the art we see,
with every ripple of effect we feel
with every ripple like some soft sound
that, like magic, continues to rebound
within our community.

Her heart beats in the poems
she wrote and shared with us—
poems of strength and poems of struggle,
poems of praise and of passion,
poems of friendship and of gratitude,
poems of love, and poems of lust
that made me blush—
Like, I mean, *damn,* Stormi!

Her heart still beats in those poems she wrote
and never shared, but kept to herself,
close to her heart.
Her heart still beats in the poets, collected here,
young and old, friends and strangers,
first-timers and old-timers,
all brought together here at the Trunk.

Her heart still beats in the chests
of the souls up here nervously reading
for the first time, and her heart's beating
in the sooth-sayers spittin' fire at the Trunk of Truth—
her heart still beats *from within*
the Trunk of Truth—
her heart beats at the Trunk.
I can feel it.

And her heart still beats in me—
the day I first came here and met her
she treated me like family I had yet to know.
Like long-lost cousins, like
it's all good, nothing wrong.
Jonie and I felt that warmth when she let us in
and made us feel like we belong.
Open arms and kind words from day one.
And that loving warmth would only grow.

And her heart still beats in the respect we show
when someone's up here at the mic,
because you sure don't want that look, like

a poetic storm raining down on you
if you're not giving the mic
the respect it's due.

Her heart still beats in you, we few who
come here together to share
this fire she lit and tended,
a fire that will never be ended,
a fire of love and unity
and respect and community.
A fire she fed with poetic fuel
like she fed us Trunk Treats—
and her heart still beats.

I can feel it.

Unsolicited Advice for Insecure People

Make love with her now
like it is the last time.
It is always the last time.

Pray that the sky marries the horizon.
Pray that the sea marries the sky.
Pray that the dust learns to weep.

Pray that those tears are nourishing.
See spring buds as red leaves,
they are. Imagine your Nana

as a little girl. Think of all those pigtails
she yanked. Of course she did. Leaves fall
each year and cover the sidewalk.

Jump when the song says jump.
Pray the sun comes back each morning.
It will come up anyway, sure, but

it's good to keep magic.
Don't walk near cliffs' edges
but walk near cliffs' edges.

So much depends upon remembering
that there is nothing after this, and then
making the most of what comes next.

Adrian Lime is a poet, spray paint artist, and UAW autoworker. A founding member of Toledo's Almeda Street Poets, he helped to launch the Toledo Poetry Museum and ToledoPoet.com. He has been published in a handful of local and national online and print journals. His first book of poetry, *Feeding the Monster* (2018, EMP Books), is a collaboration of factory poems with poet Michael Grover. Adrian works at the Toledo Jeep North Assembly plant, and lives in a nice little house in West Toledo with his wife.